LEO

LEO

Let your Sun sign show you the way
to a happy and fulfilling life

Marion Williamson & Pam Carruthers

SIRIUS

This edition published in 2021 by Sirius Publishing, a division of
Arcturus Publishing Limited,
26/27 Bickels Yard, 151–153 Bermondsey Street,
London SE1 3HA

ISBN: 978-1-3988-0860-7
AD008762UK

Printed in China

CONTENTS

Introduction

*W*elcome, Leo! You have just taken a step toward what might become a lifelong passion. When astrology gets under your skin, there's no going back. Astrology helps you understand yourself and the people around you, and its dazzling insights become more fascinating the deeper you go.

Just as the first humans turned to the life-giving Sun for sustenance and guidance, your astrological journey begins with your Sun sign of Leo. First, we delve deeply into the heart of what makes you tick, then we'll continue to unlock your cosmic potential by exploring love, your career and health, where you might prefer to live, and how you get along with family and friends.

Then it's over to gifted astrologer, Pam Carruthers, for her phenomenal birthdate analysis, where she gives personality insights for your specific Leo birthday.

In the last part of the book we get right inside how astrology works by revealing the different layers that will help you understand your own birth chart and offer the planetary tools to get you started.

Are you ready, Leo? Let's look at what makes you such a sunny, popular character!

CUSP DATES FOR LEO
23 July – 23 August

The exact time of the Sun's entry into each zodiac sign varies every year, so it's impossible to list them all. If you were born a day either side of the dates above, you're a 'cusp' baby. This means you may feel like you're a blend of Leo/Cancer or Leo/Virgo or you may instinctively just know that you're one sign right to your core.

Going deeper

If you want to know once and for all whether you're a Cancer, Leo or Virgo, you can look up your birthdate in a planetary ephemeris, of which there are plenty online. (See page 102 for more information.) This shows the exact moment the Sun moved into a new zodiac sign for the month you were born.

The Leo personality

*Y*ou are regal, dignified, courageous Leo, ruled by the life-giving creative force of the Sun. And, like the Sun, your place is at the centre of the solar system, where everything revolves around you!

In a birth chart the Sun represents the self, the ego, the personal spark of the divine, which means you need to shine. With your passionate, creative, Fire sign energy, you're full of warmth and positivity – and sparkle with life.

Commanding and authoritative, you can have a slightly condescending manner, but that's usually because you genuinely feel you know what's best for everyone. You were born to lead the pack, to encourage, protect and provide for others – so you need other people to give you a sense of purpose. Your motivation is usually to make other people happy and, yes, you can be a little bit firm in enforcing your rules sometimes, but you know you are strong and brave and that your intentions come from the heart. It's this generosity of spirit that makes you one of the most popular signs of the zodiac.

You're a true people-person and you enjoy nothing more than basking in the love you feel for others. This is one of the reasons you are attracted to the spotlight so much. Love is your reason for living. When you're the centre of attention, or on stage in some way, the applause and validation fill you with rays of joy, which you radiate back out to your admirers like a little sun.

CREATIVE CREATURE

Powered by the regenerative force of the Sun, most Leos wish to change the world for the better – and what better way than to create something beautiful? This is why Leo is the zodiac sign most associated with children, as they are the embodiment of creation. Typical Leo usually wants to start a family, but if that doesn't appeal, making something of lasting value will likely still be of paramount importance.

You were born with the talent and self-confidence to show off your skills, and you're not shy about displaying your brilliance – you see it as your gift to the Universe. But for all your swagger and bravado, you do need encouragement. Leo has to know that what they're doing is unique and wonderful and that nobody else can offer what they can. Inside every Leo there's a little innocent child, who craves love and reassurance. And when the praise comes you prefer it to be as flattering and dramatic as possible ... preferably sung from rooftops or displayed on an aeroplane banner. After all, there's not much point in making or doing something extraordinary if nobody really appreciates it. Sun-ruled people don't sit in the shadows, they confidently thrust their talents and ideas into the light of day, and bravely expect to be loved for it.

BOSSY OR JUST RIGHT?

You're an enterprising, vigorous worker who appreciates that you must put in the effort to be able to afford the good things in life. Whatever your job, you tackle it with intensity and determination and expect to be well-rewarded. You are one of the zodiac's most lavish spenders, with a penchant for luxury goods. A healthy work ethic is essential if you're to keep up with your swanky tastes and social life!

When you get your teeth into something, you're dynamic, focused and completely absorbed. You'll be directing other people, coming up with brilliant ideas and generally working yourself and everyone around you very hard.

As you are so well organised yourself, it's difficult for you to watch other people live more chaotic, less structured lives. You only want the best for your loved ones and you're so confident and self-assured, that it's very hard to resist not intervening when you think they're making a mistake.

You often find it easier to get others' lives in order, rather than concentrating on your own priorities. This is partly because it's easier for you to focus on what other people need out of a genuine concern for their welfare. But it's also because you're such a naturally extroverted character that doing things for yourself, on your own, just doesn't excite you that much.

Some of your friends and family may label this over-eagerness to help as bossiness. But you'll usually argue that you're just pushing them to be the best they can – and ignore their pleas! The thing is, Leo, you're such a wise and knowledgeable person that others will naturally gravitate toward you for advice anyway. So, if you do give people some space, they'll probably feel a little anxious that you're not going to hold their hand, and will come running back for help.

LEO TIME

It's a Leo myth that you're a 'lazy lion'. You're one the zodiac's most dedicated workers, but once the graft is done, you play, luxuriate and indulge your senses. You're an exuberant partier, with exquisite tastes. Champagne bubble baths, expensive night clubs, the finest wines known to humanity, clothes of spun gold… whatever your gender, you embody the socialite archetype.

You're actually no lazier than anyone else but because you expend so much energy working and playing, you do tend to sleep more than most. You love a lie-in and certainly enjoy being catered for. You will put in extra hours at the office if it means avoiding menial chores if you can help it. No self-respecting true Leo will look you in the eye while pulling hairs from the plughole. You'll happily hire nannies, dog walkers, cleaners, accountants and sometimes chefs to free up your precious time, leaving you to enjoy your hard-earned Leo time.

DON'T IGNORE ME!

The problem with thinking the world revolves around you, is that when there's nobody around to watch you be fabulous, you might as well be invisible. Nothing hurts you more than being ignored; after all, you're doing all this for everyone else's benefit. But it's not just that the attention isn't on you for a moment, it's more that when there's nobody else around, you're forced to focus on yourself. You're not one for self-contemplation, but that's exactly what you need from time to time because you could do with balancing out your need for external validation with some of your own healthy esteem. You must have time out from others to remember what *you* want.

You have lots of acquaintances, some of whom don't really know the real you – and you don't want to be one of them! Deep down you might be a little scared or insecure that you can't or don't actually live up to your extraordinary reputation. You can be all bluff and bluster, and you secretly fear that your roar is more impressive than your bite. When you do willingly spend some time on your own, you might be pleasantly surprised.

Take a night off and see what happens, just you, no social media and no communication with the outside world. Find out who you really are, Leo. It won't take long for your creative instinct to kick in and you'll find that making something will give you a purpose, without requiring an audience. Dressmaking, painting, collage and baking are all projects where you can share your creations with the people you love – and they'll really appreciate your generosity.

You don't often let other people see you when you're not 'on show'. You're all for false eyelashes, high fashion, sharp suits and flash cars. Your loved ones will see past your glam-armour, but perhaps you need to be a little kinder to the raw, unshaved, dressing gown and slippers, you, too. Deep down you're actually just a little pussycat asking to be loved.

AQUARIUS LESSON

Aquarius is your opposite sign of the zodiac, and in astrological terms, opposites really do attract. There's usually something alluring about your zodiac counterpart, perhaps they exude a value that you haven't fully developed in your own personality yet. Leo and Aquarius are compatible elements – Fire and Air – you need each other to survive. You're both original and stand out in some way – Aquarius in their cool, eccentric manner, and you with your glitzy attention-grabbing style.

What you secretly admire about emotionally-detached Aquarius is that they don't appear to need attention. They'd be exactly who they are alone in a cave, where you're a little terrified that you only truly come alive when there's an audience. You're more than a little in awe of Aquarius' ability to break with convention, and it both confuses and excites you that they genuinely don't give a stuff about what other people think. There's a lesson for you there, and it may take until you are much older to fully appreciate it, but Aquarius is showing you one of your life's most valuable lessons.

DARLING I'M RIGHT IN THE MIDDLE OF BEING FABULOUS – CAN YOU CALL ME BACK?

Leo in love

*L*ove is your language, Leo. As an exuberant, warm, effusive person you don't find it difficult to show your affections. You feel alive when you're attracted to someone new – you'll feel full of possibilities and puppy-like enthusiasm. You're an excellent judge of character and will normally be pretty sure that your intended will at least feel some of the excitement you're experiencing. If you're not quite sure, you will need encouragement … you're not going to make a fool of yourself for someone who's unable to return your affections.

You'll be tentative at first and if there's any uncertainty you'll hold back until you're sure you can win their heart. The slightest hint of reciprocation will light the touch-paper and then you'll gleefully pounce. You're all in for love. You don't understand why anyone would play mind-games – surely if you're both certain of one another, there's no point in pretending otherwise? More fearful or cautious zodiac signs may try to play it cool with a new lover, as they build up confidence, but when you get the green light, you want the whole world to know how happy you are.

Grand romantic gestures don't get more dramatic than a Leo in love. You take all the conventional love clichés and cover them in gold and glitter. You love like you want to be loved in return – with an adoring, ardent, unquenchable passion. Thinking you can show how much you love someone by showering them with gifts and attention, your other half will be bowled over by your generosity and care – and perhaps a little overwhelmed.

When you put so much of yourself into making your life together a fabulous, romantic adventure, you do expect your partner to reciprocate in kind. The problem here is that few people find it so natural and easy to be as generous with themselves as you. You set the bar so high that it's a lot for your lover to live up to. They might be worried about spending too much money on lavish gifts, or a little timid in expressing so much emotion.

This can be disappointing for Leo, as you crave public shows of affection. If someone loves you, they too should trumpet it from the heavens, empty their bank account and plan oodles of secret romantic trips – because that's how *you* do it – that's how love is done! You can be a hard act to follow for more modest or timid types who show their affections in a quieter, less dramatic way. And you have to learn that love can be deep and passionate without everything being for show.

PLAY TOGETHER, STAY TOGETHER

Togetherness is hugely important for you in a relationship. You can accept if your other half has other obligations and responsibilities, as long as your time together is spent doing something interesting. Shared pastimes are vital, so finding someone with a matched love for drama and entertainment would be a big plus. Getting excited about the same things, whether that's frequent trips to the movies, attending dance classes or a love of cosplay will fuel your need for fun and togetherness.

After the passion cools to a steadier sizzle, you'll be concerned if your lover is happy to sit at home watching TV every night. You want to be seen and heard, preferably dressed up to the nines at a millionaire's yacht party or at an exclusive casino!

TRICKY EMOTIONS

What other people think of your partner is a big issue. If friends or family disapprove, you'll do your best to win them over by over-emphasising their good points or making them out to be more glamorous than they are – or want to be. This tendency to gloss over or embellish the more mundane aspects of your life together can make your partner feel that they're not living up to your expectations – or being allowed to be who they are.

You are extremely proud of your partner, and want to show them off, and see their behaviour and appearance as inextricably linked to your own personality. So, when your adored chooses to be themselves, happy to spend all day reading or tinkering with their car, you can feel ignored and alone – two emotions you're really uncomfortable with.

You are loving, supportive and generous in your relationships but you probably need to learn that being alone together and making each other happy is more important than what your adoring public see.

Most compatible love signs

Libra – what a glamorous, charming pair – you both know how to impress other people and love being the centre of attention.

Sagittarius – You're the two most generous people in the zodiac. You'll have heaps of fun and enjoy emptying your joint bank account together!

Gemini – the sparkling entertainment team is here, and neither of you will get a wink of sleep when the other is around.

Least compatible love signs

Leo – you can get jealous when there's another big cat on the scene, stealing all the limelight.

Scorpio – lots of passion initially, but Scorpio's broody emotions and shady game-playing is too underhand for an upfront Leo.

Capricorn – Goat people are not usually emotionally demonstrative, which will cool your need for praise super-fast.

Leo at work

On a deep level you respect that if you are to enjoy the best things in life, you need to work solidly for them. Your perfect job is one where you can shine and be admired, while making oodles of cash. You want to bring people joy and pleasure, and to be heartily rewarded and thanked for your efforts. You sometimes can have so much fun at work that it can appear that you're not stressed out or worried enough to be doing it right. But you actually rival Virgo for being the most organised sign of the zodiac.

You are reliable, responsible and loyal and have a natural ability to take control of any situation, and your healthy self-esteem commands the respect of your colleagues. You'll have your eye on the top job but need to watch that your ego doesn't rub co-workers the wrong way. Your need for attention and praise can mean you need to remember to let more unassuming personalities have their time in the spotlight.

LOOK WHAT I DID!

As one of the most creative and artistic signs of the zodiac, finding work that's an extension of your self-expression, would be an ideal fit. Whether you are offering gorgeous artwork, cooking wonderful food or crafting unique furniture, you need to be proud of your accomplishments and feel that they enhance other people's lives too.

You are happiest in a position where you can stand by your work and proudly declare, "I did that!"

Working in a job where there are not many opportunities to shine or progress wilts you, and undermines your self-confidence. You actually need a good deal of encouragement, especially when you're in a new position. You thrive when you have an audience, so working on your own or behind the scenes is not ideal, unless there's a regular award or prize on offer for your achievements.

WELL DONE, LEO

You excel in any position where the focus is on you. Acting is often described as the perfect job for Leo because it involves performing in the spotlight, receiving applause, and adopting a glamorous public image. The entertainment industry has a magnetic pull for Leo looking for the limelight, and singing, dancing or a career in music will be high on your list.

You love a touch of drama, so you excel in careers that allow your daring, extroverted nature to roam free. But even in less glam industries, when you're excited about what you're doing, you'll enthusiastically extol the virtues of your wonderful project, exclusive shop, exciting department or unbeatable team. People who are wise to your susceptibility to flattery can take advantage a little. For example, you may be pleased to accept an extravagant job title in place of a pay hike or be credited for something that doesn't matter in the grand scheme of things. Flashy diversion tactics may distract you for a while, but you're no fool. You always had your eyes on the top job – and that's naturally where you're headed.

KING OF THE JUNGLE

Leo takes charge instinctively, so being where the buck stops is where you are most comfortable. Magnanimous or tyrannical, there'll be no mistaking who's in charge. You're a fearless decision maker, calm in a crisis – and the people working for you respect and trust your judgement.

Your love of showing people what to do and encouraging them to grow makes you a popular boss. A patient teacher, you want others to appreciate your wisdom and experience, and to show some gratitude for your efforts. In return, you are generous and reward loyalty handsomely. It's champagne all round when you're celebrating success and you thoroughly enjoy watching people bask in the benefits you provide as the leader of the pack. Acutely aware of the need for downtime, you're happy to see your employees let their hair down when they've been working hard. You're the kind of boss who, as long as nobody questions your authority, is happy to let your team finish early on a Friday or take a longer lunch on occasion.

Most compatible colleagues

Taurus – loyal, consistent and hard-working, Taurus and Leo work towards the same goals – the finer things in life.

Leo – you both work and play well together but you will have to share the spotlight.

Sagittarius – as a team, your vision and creativity is breathtaking but you'll need someone who's more practical on board, too.

Least compatible colleagues

Virgo – these guys think of everything, but they spend too much time agonising over tiny details.

Capricorn – takes work very seriously and never seems to enjoy it. You're no workaholic and your downtime is crucial.

Pisces – your upfront, noisy, brash approach alarms Pisces who needs a tranquil quiet space.

Perfect **Leo Careers**

Actor

Opera singer

Influencer

Fashion designer

Circus ringmaster

Comedian

Cruise ship entertainer

Cardiologist

Traffic warden

Jewellery designer

Leo
Work Motto

I'M NOT BOSSY, I JUST KNOW WHAT YOU SHOULD BE DOING.

Leo friends and family

*F*or all your outward-leaning popularity, you are actually a little cautious about calling someone your friend, and you're suspicious of anyone who assumes your friendship without getting to know you well. You love meeting new people and have an unusually large circle of acquaintances, but for you to declare that someone is more than an admiring hanger-on is another matter. This is partly because you feel a sense of responsibility as the leader of the group to look out for your friends – and there are only so many people you can squeeze under your wing. You also spend a great deal of time, money and energy on the people you care about, so you tend to choose wisely.

Once you so decide someone is your buddy, you'll do everything in your power to be there for them. A naturally encouraging person, you'll give moral support when they need to feel brave, and a shoulder to cry on when they need you. You're not just a trustworthy, loyal companion, you have quite the reputation for being a party animal. Nobody goes for a quiet night out with Leo. You love dancing, music, extravagant shows and cabarets, theatre, fancy restaurants and glamorous clothes. You'll encourage everyone around you to overindulge and you'll all have a laugh about your over-the-top antics the next day.

FAMILY PRIDE

Your home is your royal lair, your kingdom, and as a Sun-ruled person you'll like it to be filled with natural light. Potted plants, herbs and leafy flower displays will appeal, as will oversized or ostentatious furniture and some exotic touches. You are an extravagant decorator preferring bold colours and patterns and some original fine art will usually be on display.

An inviting den will be the heart of your home, whether you have a large family or a pet pussycat. A little vain, you may choose to display a flattering portrait of yourself, and you'll highlight any pictures of your loved ones at boastful moments – graduating, performing or meeting famous people.

You want everyone under your roof to be happy and see it as your responsibility to keep them all content and entertained. Home entertaining is your forte, gathering loved ones around for grand dinner parties. You love to show off your expensive taste and treat everyone to the finest fare you can afford.

LEO PARENT

A proud parent, you adore watching your children grow, explore and build confidence. You're fiercely protective of your youngsters and will see it as your job to shower them with all the love and attention you're capable of – nothing is too good for your child. You expect loyalty and obedience in return and can feel very hurt if your offspring don't appreciate your sacrifice. But love always wins the day for Leo – a hug and some kind words work like magic, and all will be forgiven.

LEO CHILD

Fire sign, Leo children usually get what they want. When in a good mood they are like little rays of sunlight, delightful, entertaining and eager to please, like a cute little lion cub. But when they think they're not getting enough attention, those little rays of sunlight can turn into scorching laser beams. Ignore your little Leo at your peril, as they're happy to push the boundaries and engage in power battles to find out who's really the boss. When they get older your Leo kid may enjoy dressing outlandishly or, a born performer, putting on shows for friends and family.

Healthy Leo

R uled by the life-giving Sun, you're a high-energy person with an unquenchable zest for life. You take your exercise routine seriously, partly because you're a Fire sign, and will feel more relaxed when you've burned off some of that excess zeal – but typically it's vanity that is your biggest motivator, and you know it keeps you looking so good!

Vigorous workouts and cardio routines keep your circulatory system ticking over, but you would rather be outside in the sun and fresh air than cooped up in a gym or sports club. You can't keep a lion indoors for long – unless they're sleeping.

Having the undivided attention of a personal trainer might be something that's hard to resist as you'll be happy to impress someone who is there exclusively to encourage and praise you. An expert to help with your dietary requirements and a specially-tailored meal plan would also gratify your need for attention, and your own personal chef would be perfect!

TEAM LEO

Fun and games are a favourite Leo pastime, whether playing cards or Monopoly at home, or enjoying a vigorous sporting challenge where you can improve on your personal best, with activities like golf, tennis or interval training.

You're happiest when surrounded by other people, so being a member of a team will satisfy your social instincts. Football, basketball, hockey and most team sports will appeal, and, of course, you will aim to be the star player. You expect applause and praise but it's really your enthusiastic spirited approach and great organisational skills that make you such a valued player.

FLAMBOYANT TASTE

If you could afford it, you'd probably choose to eat out most of the time. You get to show off your new outfit, talk to everyone and get seen in a fashionable dining spot. Besides, cooking and cleaning isn't really your thing. You do enjoy baking awesome-looking cakes because of the wow factor, but you'll leave all the washing up to someone else. Your expertise lies in drama, not drudgery.

You prefer eating in company and your generosity and flamboyant taste make you a perfect dinner date. When you choose something from the menu, you're usually looking for the caviar, lobsters and oysters rather than anything modest or that you probably have in your own fridge back home. You'll plump for the fanciest dish on the menu, and insist on buying everyone at the table drinks.

BIG CAT DOWNTIME

Relaxing is a big deal for you, but even your downtime can look pretty hectic to less energetic types. As the zodiac's favourite party animal, when you're out having fun you'll be on your feet until the music stops, you run out of alcohol, or everyone else leaves. But lions need their sleep and you can get tetchy if you haven't had a proper lie-in for a few days. You can occasionally appear lazy – but if anyone sees what you've been doing the rest of the time, they'll understand why you're anything but!

BODY AREA: HEART AND SPINE

The sign of Leo governs the heart, symbolising the lion's courage and bravery. The spine is also associated with Leo and most people of this sign tend to stick their chests out proudly and exhibit something of a leonine strut.

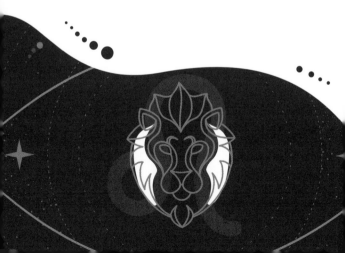

Leo on the move

*A*ttracted to ritzy, glitzy locations and glamorous surroundings, wherever you're going, you're going there in style. You demand the best travel options you can afford, and you'll travel first class when you can.

Regal lions don't want to spend their precious vacation time walking to bus stops or waiting around in chilly train stations. Forking out the extra cash on taxis, cars and VIP treatment is worth every penny if it's a more comfortable or enjoyable option. Face it, Leo, you'd have your own private jet if you had half the chance!

You'll be the one making all the decisions about where you're going but you'll need someone else to take care of the less interesting details. Bookings, schedules and the practicalities of packing, are best left to another, more methodical travel companion. Though you will have planned exactly what you're going to wear on your journey and know how to strut through an airport like a rock star.

INDULGENT AND DELIGHTFUL

You're a gregarious glamour-puss at heart, and you're not spending all that money and effort to go hiking or camping. You'll save money if it means travelling to a fancier hotel or a more exotic location. Big cities with plenty of nightlife, unique dining options and world-class entertainment, is where you'll fit right in. You want to interact with the beautiful people and you revel in seeing others at their best. Limelight-loving Leo wants to be at the most ostentatious places with the most interesting people, eating the most divine food.

A true Leo prefers warm countries to cooler ones, as you love the feel of the sun on your skin. And you're drawn to glamorous resorts on the French Riviera, the extravagant luxury of Dubai or dancing all night at the swankiest clubs in Ibiza. Sensual, luxurious spas, rooftop infinity pools and fabulous hotel rooms all remind you that you are the zodiac's royalty.

GOOD COMPANY

Your Fire sign company-loving personality needs at least one good friend – or preferably an entourage – with whom to share your adventures. Family trips can be good fun too, as long as someone is assigned to be the designated driver or sensible person. Never boring and always dramatic, every day away with you is a constant escapade. You will out-drink, out-dance and out-glam everyone, while looking like you've just stepped out of a movie set, even at 4 o'clock in the morning.

Of course, there's no point in being at all these amazing places if nobody knows you are there, so you will naturally record every thrilling moment on your many social media accounts.

Leo
Favourite Places

Five-star hotels

Los Angeles

Palace of Versailles

The Sphinx

Beverley Hills

Exclusive yacht party

Rio de Janeiro

Las Vegas

Luxury spa

Theatre

Discover your
personal forecast
for the day of
your birth.

23 July

*Y*ou are an enthusiastic person, exuberant and full of life. You exude confidence and have a convincing manner about you. You can dazzle people with your brilliance and always need to command centre stage. You take the lead without being asked – it just seems right. You have an almost mythic life with wonderful opportunities falling into your lap, which can make others envious as you seem to be successful without even trying. In relationships you need an enormous amount of affection and admiration. You can dominate your environment and are not always that easy to live with. At times you are just too hot to handle and you need to cool down and learn to appreciate others more. You are an exhibitionist, so entertaining others will give them pleasure and help you burn off some of your excess energy.

STRENGTHS
Cheerful and full
of positivity

WEAKNESSES
A constant need for
attention, and a showoff

MEDITATION
*Don't underestimate the
power of the understatement.*

24 July

*Y*ou are a dedicated and articulate person who inspires others with your desire for excellence. You are kind and warm and you come across to people as supremely self-confident. However, there is an inner voice which is less sure and is always criticizing whatever you do or say. Your biggest weakness is that you tend to over-analyse yourself and others. Professionally you work best alone or freelance – you can contribute to a team but groups do not interest you much. You work well with detail and can spend hours perfecting your creations. You are very fussy when it comes to relationships; you need someone who is willing to shower you with affection, and put up with your idiosyncrasies. You can get edgy, so watch your diet and avoid eating too many spicy foods.

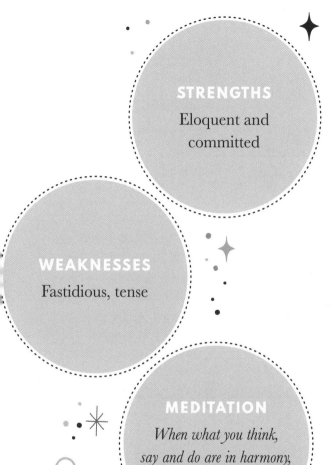

STRENGTHS
Eloquent and
committed

WEAKNESSES
Fastidious, tense

MEDITATION
*When what you think,
say and do are in harmony,
happiness will come.*

25 July

You are a soft and loving person with innate qualities of the diplomat. You see the world – maybe a little naively – as a place of harmony, and you bring sweetness and sparkle just by your presence. You cannot help but win attention from others as you have an aura that glows with a deep sense of peace and happiness. You were well brought up, and your manners are flawless. You like things to be in the right place and have a strong sense of design and artistic talent. You can succeed in the areas of illustration, interior design and floristry. Your home always looks beautiful with your impeccable good taste. You long for romance and seek a partner who has a strong sense of identity. Sugary foods can be your downfall – your need for sweetness is really a need for love.

STRENGTHS
Affectionate, creative

WEAKNESSES
Mawkish and
sweet-toothed

MEDITATION
*We're fools whether
we dance or not, so
we might as well dance.*

26 July

*Y*ou are a magnetic and attractive person with a powerful presence. You have a true star quality, a strong sense of purpose and the determination to win at all costs. You never give up on yourself and your ambition has no limits. You have tremendous willpower and once at the top you can beat off all competition. Relationships are vital for you and you will often have more than one true love. The aura of mystery emanating from you is extremely seductive. You are fiercely loyal to your loved ones and yet your partners feel they never really understand you. Your need for secrecy holds you back from real intimacy. Learn to trust more and open up. You love murder mysteries and thrillers, so time out for you at the theatre or cinema is a favourite way to relax.

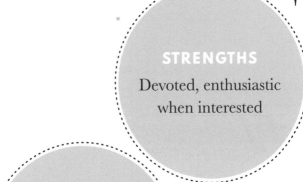

STRENGTHS
Devoted, enthusiastic
when interested

WEAKNESSES
Ruthless and secretive

MEDITATION
*Try not to become a person
of success, but rather a
person of value.*

27 July

You are a person with a positive outlook on all that life has to offer; someone who has an immense belief deep inside that life is meant to be an adventure and lived to the full. You explore the world, either literally or in your imagination. You have a wanderlust that lasts all your life and you can take a long time to settle down, if indeed you do. You are incredibly warm and generous – a real party person – and offer kindness to everyone you meet. You have high moral standards and defend the truth, so are naturally attracted to the legal professions. The courtroom suits your large personality. You are a rolling stone so a full-time relationship can be difficult, but you value your partner's friendship highly. You love to learn, so home study will keep you occupied and satisfy your restless spirit.

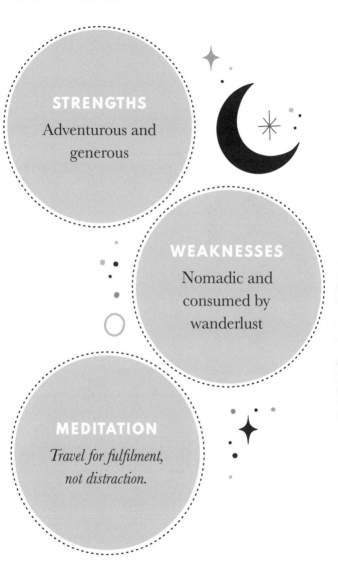

STRENGTHS
Adventurous and generous

WEAKNESSES
Nomadic and consumed by wanderlust

MEDITATION
Travel for fulfilment, not distraction.

28 July

You are a formidable and ambitious person with a positive manner, yet you are basically quite shy. The support of older people helps you throughout your life. You develop a self-controlled polish as you get older, and you love formality and grand functions. You long for a bygone era when good manners and traditions were valued. You are always respected but can remain dazzlingly aloof to some, so developing compassion would benefit you. You get to the top, whether on your own or with a partner. It is a position that you are well suited to. You also make a loyal partner and marriage flatters you, as you crave material security and a stable home. Working fulfils you, but you also need to laugh and have fun more often or you'll get old before your time.

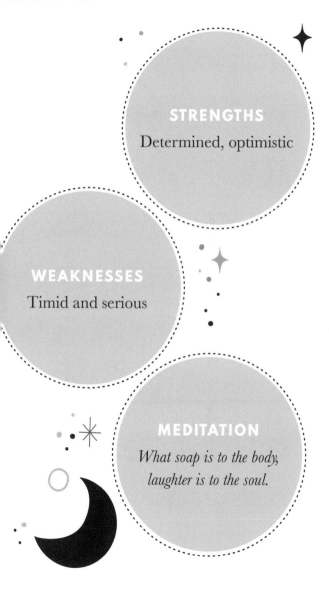

STRENGTHS
Determined, optimistic

WEAKNESSES
Timid and serious

MEDITATION
*What soap is to the body,
laughter is to the soul.*

29 July

*Y*ou are an innovative leader who does things in your own inimitable style. You are resourceful and are willing to try out new methods, the more whacky the better, and are never put off if things don't go according to plan! You are truly inventive and can go to extremes in what you are prepared to do. The problem is your lack of perspective, and you can be very resistant to change once you have decided on a course of action. You aim to include people and, as long as you are the boss, you work well in a team. In relation-ships you want both a best friend and someone to look up to you. You have a love/hate affair with technology and need to switch off at night as your mind gets over-active. Going for a walk – without your mobile phone – will help you to unwind.

STRENGTHS
Original, enterprising

WEAKNESSES
Stubborn and
domineering

MEDITATION
*The best remedy for a short
temper is a long walk.*

30 July

*Y*ou are a strong and lively person with a gift of humour. You have a warm spontaneity about you and a playful way with words, which means that you can come out with the perfect one-liner at exactly the right time. You can be the clown, and yet you never look foolish or lose your innate self-confidence. Your quick wit and intelligence is engaging and you are a popular leader. You are the perfect host or dinner party guest as you keep people entertained with the latest gossip. You are well-meaning and honourable, and speak from the heart. Although you like to be in charge, you never take yourself too seriously. In romance you have a penchant for variety and are inclined to make sure you are always very busy to avoid relating on a deep level. Your temperament is Fire/Air so avoid icy drinks as they can upset you.

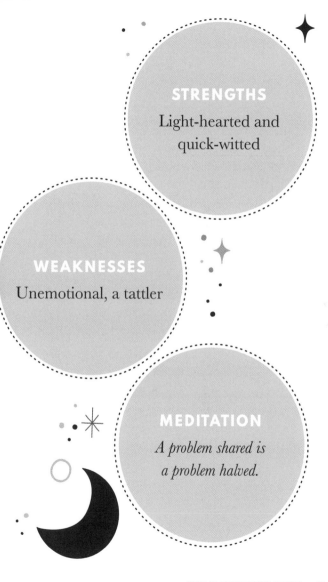

STRENGTHS
Light-hearted and
quick-witted

WEAKNESSES
Unemotional, a tattler

MEDITATION
*A problem shared is
a problem halved.*

31 July

*Y*ou are a person with a big heart who cares deeply for your family and home life. You express yourself dramatically and playfully. You have natural charisma and are good at promoting yourself to others in a genuine way. You do well in the world of show business where you shine brightly. You had a close relationship with your mother/ mother-figure and needed a lot of care and affection. Later in life you carry that inner security within you and create a home wherever you go. You tend to settle down early, are a dependable partner and provide emotional security to those you love. On the negative side, you can be too self-absorbed and over-react when criticized, although your natural warm-heartedness means you never sulk for long. Playing with your children is always a way to stop being too introspective.

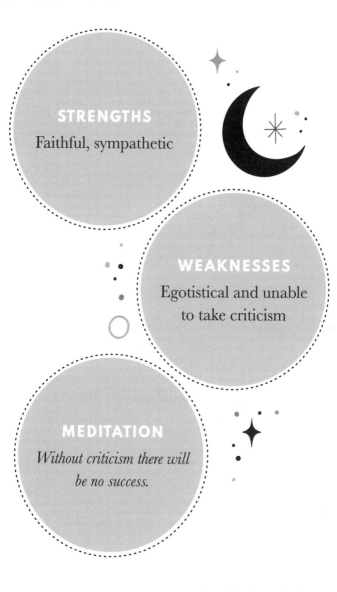

STRENGTHS

Faithful, sympathetic

WEAKNESSES

Egotistical and unable
to take criticism

MEDITATION

*Without criticism there will
be no success.*

1 August

Y ou are a passionate and creative person with strong and vibrant leadership qualities. You are intuitive and fiery, with a lot to express and give to the world. Your self-confidence is such that you know – not believe – you are the centre of the universe and have a group of adoring followers who simply love you and everything you have to offer. You are talented, love drama and are well suited to the stage. You have innate courage and will risk all for what you believe in. You also have a very tender side and are re-lationship orientated. You give wholeheartedly to your partner and you are very chivalrous. You can be too self-centred and need to have someone by your side to bring you back down to earth. You can easily burn yourself out and need someone around to remind you to take better care of yourself.

STRENGTHS

Brave and romantic

WEAKNESSES

Self-absorbed,
an exhibitionist

MEDITATION

*Too much time spent on
yourself means you will miss
the greatness of others.*

2 August

*Y*ou are a charismatic and magnetic person with a love for splendour and magnificence. You take great delight in creating a lifestyle in which you can enjoy the good things in life. You have a touch of the showman about you. Your flamboyant and glamorous personality are reflected in your taste at home – gilded mirrors, thick metallic blankets, flowers and fur. Gold is your favourite colour – and you love real gold, too. You are a creative person who can produce things that people want, whether that's an artistic experience or an exquisitely hand-made chocolate. You need a reliable mate, someone beautiful and who always matches your style. You can be stubborn and tend to see things from your point of view so need to learn to be more flexible. You love perfume – a deliciously scented bath is ideal to relax you.

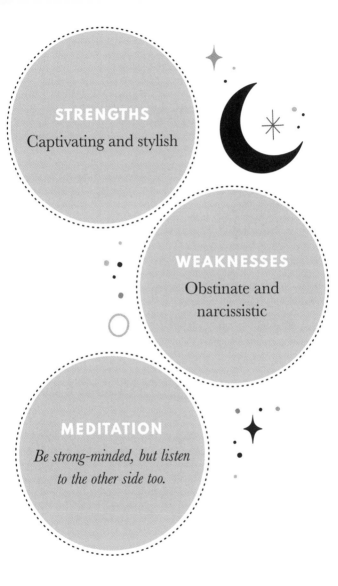

STRENGTHS

Captivating and stylish

WEAKNESSES

Obstinate and
narcissistic

MEDITATION

*Be strong-minded, but listen
to the other side too.*

3 August

*Y*ou are a youthful and optimistic person out of whom a message of hope and positivity shines. You are persuasive and believe in causes with all of your heart. You can be a political activist, and you like to move in influential circles. You need to be admired for the work you do. You are a perennial student in the sense that you love to try out new things. However, you can find it hard to focus on just one thing at a time. You need a partner to be your ally and loyal supporter as opposed to someone who will challenge you. At times you can appear naive and childlike, and this emotional immaturity can play havoc with your relationships. Humour is your saving grace and can lift you up when things get tough. When the blues descend, keep to yourself and watch a comedy until your mood changes.

STRENGTHS
Sanguine, compelling

WEAKNESSES
Emotionally naive, superficial

MEDITATION
It is better to have loved and lost than never to have loved at all.

4 August

*Y*ou are a big personality with enormous presence and a strong sense of purpose. You have an aristocratic bearing but also the rare gift of being able to reach out to others. Everyone you meet feels your warmth and included in your circle of influence. You make a truly excellent leader because imbued in you are the protective qualities of a good father as well as the emotional depth of a good mother. On the debit side you can get moody if things do not go your way. In early life you may cling to your mother and need her physical presence to feel safe. You view a loving relationship as something to commit to for life, and you are perfectly content to relax at home with the family. You can get irritable and impatient if your creativity isn't expressed. Singing helps you to let off steam.

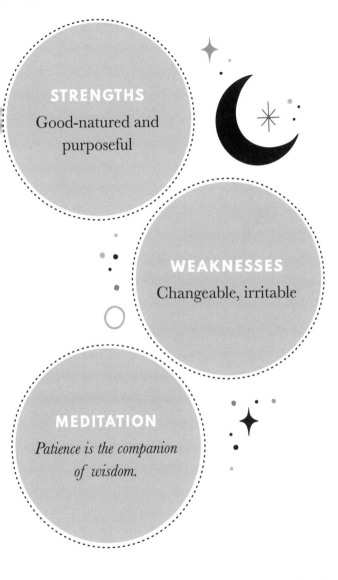

STRENGTHS
Good-natured and
purposeful

WEAKNESSES
Changeable, irritable

MEDITATION
*Patience is the companion
of wisdom.*

5 August

*Y*ou are a magnetic and warm-hearted person whose life is a journey of self-discovery. You are an inspiration and give yourself totally to whatever endeavour you get involved with. You are best suited to being in a managerial or executive role and do not take kindly to being in a menial position. You are hopeless at detail – it just doesn't interest you. You radiate out into the world and to be successful you need others to appreciate you. Be mindful that your ego can be overwhelming and you need to give other people some time in the limelight. Your passionate nature can lead to temptation in relationships; if your partner doesn't adore you constantly, you'll swap them for someone who does. The theatre is a wonderful arena for you, and amateur dramatics is a way to get your needs met.

STRENGTHS

Captivating and
inspirational

WEAKNESSES

Self-important,
overbearing

MEDITATION

*Let others make their
own mistakes and
their own successes.*

6 August

*Y*ou are an ethical and rigorous person with strongly held ideals. However, even though you know deep down what you think, you have a tendency to hesitate and procrastinate. You notice all the flaws in a project and want to remedy them – you need an external deadline otherwise nothing would ever be finished. Once you focus, though, you go for it and produce an excellent end result. You are benevolent and find true fulfilment when in service to others. You make a good teacher and researcher, in particular in the health industry, and you are happy to work alone. In relationships you are choosy; you want someone who cares about their health and watches what they eat. A detox you could do together would be beneficial for you both and also help satisfy your need for self-discipline.

STRENGTHS
Kind-hearted and
virtuous

WEAKNESSES
Time-wasting,
perfectionist

MEDITATION
*Better to do something
imperfectly than to do
nothing flawlessly.*

7 August

Y   ou have immense charm and grace. You love luxury and the finer things in life. You could have a successful career in selling or PR; your warm and engaging personality could easily sway people into buying whatever you offered them. A genuine desire to see others happy makes you a perfect hostess. In return they give you the recognition you need. There is a danger of you getting too wrapped up in yourself when alone, so spending time with others is important. You need a partner, and your ideal mate would appreciate entertaining as much as you do. You are not a loner, so could run a business in partnership with your spouse. If ignored, you soon send out distress signals. Rather than having to keep asking for attention, give your love and energy to a partner who shares your fear of neglect.

STRENGTHS
Elegant and lovable

WEAKNESSES
An attention seeker, extravagant

MEDITATION
Sticks in a bundle are unbreakable.

8 August

*Y*ou are a highly competitive person who needs a sense of danger to feel really alive. You are entranced by challenge and constantly create life and death dramas that you have to overcome. You are incredibly passionate with strong desires and ideals. You automatically take command in a crisis and people respect you as the number one. You do, however, have the tendency to be stubborn and possessive and won't let go of a project even when others advise you to do so. You bring intensity to all your relationships; they are never dull. Even if you stray you expect your mate to give you unquestioning loyalty. You can remain an elusive, enigmatic personality; it would take a lifetime to unravel your complexity. Your emotions can take over, so the tranquillity of water, especially the ocean, calms you.

STRENGTHS

Commanding and
enthusiastic

WEAKNESSES

Overdramatic,
obstinate

MEDITATION

*Don't make a mountain
out of a molehill, there are
enough real peaks to climb.*

9 August

You are an enthusiastic person with strong opinions and a love of storytelling. You travel a great deal and prefer going on adventurous expeditions to regular holidays. You are never still for a minute and are always seeking out new and wonderful experiences. Your aim is to lead a life of mythical proportions – one that people will remember. You take huge risks and love to gamble. You enjoy living on the edge and you are very exciting to be around – you could have an excellent career teaching dangerous sports. In relationships your demands and excessive energy constantly test the patience of your partner. You can't bear to be ordinary, which can make you a challenging person to live with. You need to learn to reflect more. Tuning into your body with yoga would be hugely relaxing.

STRENGTHS
Dynamic and ebullient

WEAKNESSES
Insistent, a risk-taker

MEDITATION
By all means take risks,
but sprinkle them with sense.

10 August

*Y*ou are a highly gifted person, a professional with unique capabilities. You have a natural lust for life and take a bold approach to all you do. Proud of your achievements, you need to be honoured with certificates, a university degree or a seat on the board. Although you enjoy parties, you are also perfectly happy with your own company. You possess enormous dignity but your pride can be hurt if people don't show you respect or – even worse – if they laugh at you. You won't show your hurt; your self-control sees to that. You adore romance and are extravagant with your partner, showering affection on them. Looks matter, and you need someone who is both attractive and worthy of your respect. You need to let your defences down so playing silly games is an antidote to your seriousness.

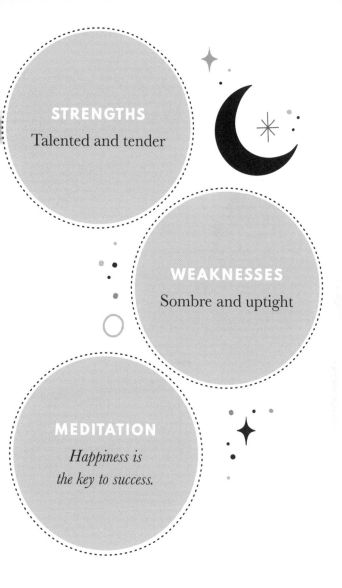

STRENGTHS
Talented and tender

WEAKNESSES
Sombre and uptight

MEDITATION
*Happiness is
the key to success.*

11 August

*Y*ou are an original, a person with a delicious sense of the ridiculous and whimsy. You have a fertile imagination and will experiment with unusual, yet inspired, combinations. You stand out in a group as the one with creative flair and will naturally be elected to lead. In politics you are a radical and will rebel against the status quo. But, however far you are from the majority, you still want people to respect you and treat you like a king or queen. You can be infuriating when you are unwilling to listen to other people's points of view. In relationships you need closeness and affection but also space and personal freedom. Travelling with your work, so you are not constantly at home, keeps your relationship alive and stops boredom setting in. However, be aware of overworking; let others care for you every once in a while.

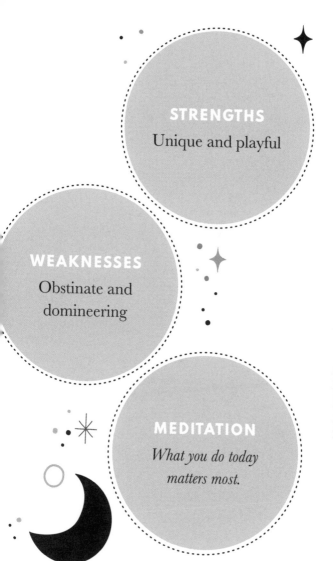

STRENGTHS
Unique and playful

WEAKNESSES
Obstinate and
domineering

MEDITATION
*What you do today
matters most.*

12 August

*Y*ou are a poetic person with an extraordinary imagination. You are in touch with the highest inspiration and express it through art, music or writing. You are intensely romantic, possibly a creative genius, and can be totally absorbed and lost for hours when the muse takes over. You are deeply touched and delighted when your art is appreciated. You enjoy partying with fellow artistic types and you need to exhibit what you produce. Your biggest joy is when others understand and share your vision. But you can fall in love with unsuitable people, because you are gullible and can be taken in by a sob story. At times you can be despondent and oversensitive to the moods of others. That is when meditation and time alone is essential for your soul. Sitting near, and gazing out at, water restores your equilibrium.

STRENGTHS

Creative and
compassionate

WEAKNESSES

Prone to dejection,
too trusting

MEDITATION

Trust only movement.
Life happens at the level of
events, not of words.

13 August

You are a congenial and confident person with an immense sense of fun. You are determined to produce and create things that everyone enjoys. This ability means you can connect with adults and children alike. You have a strong sense of identity and often follow in your father's footsteps. You are approachable and welcome people into your inner circle where you love to be the centre of attention. You seek a partner who is equal in status to you, because you like to show them off. In a relationship you can share your feelings and yet still be strong. You are a devoted partner and parent. You can exhaust yourself because you feel you have to entertain people all the time. Let them know when you need time out. An appetizing dinner at a good restaurant will help you to bounce back fast.

STRENGTHS
Friendly and
personable

WEAKNESSES
Egotistical and a bit of
a show-off

MEDITATION
*Looking at the mirror
distracts one's attention
from the problem.*

14 August

You are a giving person with a huge personality that lights up the world. Full of sunshine and love, you share yourself with all and sundry – however, you are easily flattered and so find it hard to see when people are trying to use you. You are an individualist and treat life as a play with you in the leading role; as long as you are in the spotlight all is well in your world. This contradiction in your nature can confuse those around you. In relationships you need to be the star, so do well with a partner who is willing to be back stage but hugely supportive. You can be too self-centred, and if you don't get what you want you can indulge in a temper tantrum. Your fiery energy needs expression. One way for you to lighten up is by playing charades, where everyone gets a chance to shine.

STRENGTHS

Magnanimous, caring

WEAKNESSES

Self-obsessed and
short-tempered

MEDITATION

*If you kick a stone in anger,
you'll hurt your own foot.*

15 August

*Y*ou are a radiant and hearty person with a robust sense of humour. You are self-contained to the point where you can appear aloof at times. You need a stage and will patiently work towards a position of being in the centre. People look up to you and admire your perseverance and integrity. Constant seeking to improve yourself can make you too analytical. You are very moral and have a prudent side. In your relationships you need to be in charge; your household can appear to be run like a well-oiled machine. The overly critical side of your nature can block your creativity. Nevertheless, you are still a superb artisan and fine craftsman, which is where your attention to detail is an asset. A sport – such as golf – which allows you to demonstrate your skill will help steady your sometimes skittish temperament.

STRENGTHS
Joyful and honest

WEAKNESSES
Jittery, a nit-picker

MEDITATION
Nothing in life is to be feared. It is only to be understood.

16 August

You are an expressive and outgoing person with a compelling and noble presence. Generally, you have a very positive outlook on your own life and on the lives of others, and always see the best in people. You have a unique style and a luminous quality, with a boundless zest for life. People gravitate towards you and choose you to lead the way. You can come across as imperious; you will always delegate unpleasant tasks to others. At times you are controversial and provocative. You can deliberately stir things up as you enjoy a heated debate of opposing views. You revel in relationships and will choose a partner who likes to spar with you; you enjoy the making up after a fight, but don't overdo the rows. If you give back to others the flattery you so love to receive, the resulting tenderness will reward you.

STRENGTHS

Demonstrative, with unlimited energy

WEAKNESSES

Feisty, overbearing

MEDITATION

Like nature, develop power and success from a calm centre.

17 August

*Y*ou are a dramatic and mysterious person with a quiet yet commanding demeanour. You are brilliantly creative and can trigger deep emotions in people. You are fascinating to watch – you move with a magnetism that is hypnotic. You are dynamic and forceful, yet can't be rushed or pushed by others. Your need to win makes you a poor loser, and you will often resort to manipulative temper tantrums to get your way. People can be in awe of you and sense that you need to be given space. Your relationships can be tumultuous because of your excessive jealousy. The big scenes you create can become very tiring for partners – give them a break and learn to master your emotions. Your stress levels can be high and drumming would be a fabulous way to release your energy.

STRENGTHS
Quietly confident
and imaginative

WEAKNESSES
Unsporting, distrustful

MEDITATION
*Being a fair player makes
the only real winner.*

18 August

*Y*ou are an expressive and outspoken person who has a strong desire to use the example of their own life to teach people how to expand their minds and explore what the world has to offer. You cannot be limited and have to give full rein to your creativity and vision – which is big. You love horses and the wildness of the Outback, and feel most alive when roaming across wide open spaces. A brilliant raconteur, your stories have a moral to them. You love with a passion and are very dramatic, but your tendency not to commit to a long-term relationship suggests that you avoid deep emotions. You could have many romances until you meet your intellectual equal, who will keep you on your toes. Staying still is difficult for you, and burn out is a real danger if you neglect to eat and rest. Superfoods and vitamins will support you.

STRENGTHS

An adventurer,
a true visionary

WEAKNESSES

A roamer, outspoken

MEDITATION

*Silence is the true friend
that never betrays.*

19 August

*Y*ou are a bright star, someone who will make a mark on the world for a long time and from a very early age. You have a natural charisma and charm that both men and women adore; you make them feel special and in turn they respond by giving you whatever you want. You desire power and status and will work long hours to achieve success. You exude an aura of confidence but in your youth can be self-questioning and doubt your ability. You have very high standards of excellence and set tests for others. You view relationships as serious and enduring, and whatever happens between you and a partner you'll stay and sort it out. You can be vain and seduced by flattery. Your gifts of leadership are well used when you donate time to helping others. A social sport such as golf would help you unwind.

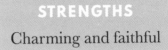

STRENGTHS
Charming and faithful

WEAKNESSES
Self-admiring,
power hungry

MEDITATION
*Power only follows respect
for others and for oneself.*

20 August

Y ou are a generous and sincere person with an expressive, almost theatrical, personality. You know what you want in life and set yourself a series of goals in order to achieve it. You have good financial common sense and in business you know what makes sense commercially. You have a large appetite for life and are very talented. You can achieve success in whatever you turn your hand to. You would do well in the fashion business when it is your name on the label. You can, however, be quite scathing and forthright in your opinions, yet people still love you. You need to shine and be adored. You don't take criticism well. Your relationships matter to you. You are an intensely amorous lover with a tactile nature. Keeping a pet you can stroke is a lovely way to keep you relaxed.

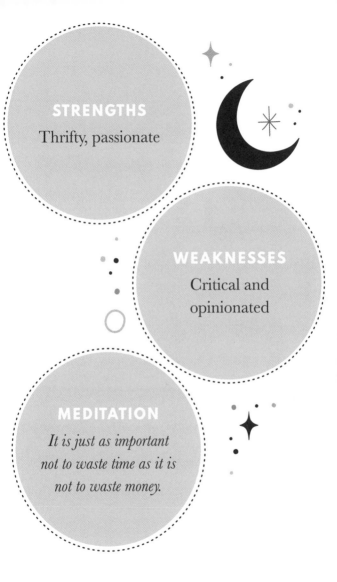

STRENGTHS
Thrifty, passionate

WEAKNESSES
Critical and
opinionated

MEDITATION
*It is just as important
not to waste time as it is
not to waste money.*

21 August

*Y*ou are a light-hearted inquisitive person who is very adaptable and ambitious. You have well-developed communication skills and are both resourceful and a quick learner. You have a strong sense of honour combined with flexibility. Although you like to be in the leadership position, you don't care for hierarchy. You excel at creative writing. You appeal to children and the young at heart. In romance it is hard to pin you down; you can be like a butterfly, always moving around. You are a born narcissist and need many people to adore you. Your partner can nudge you if you get too pompous. Your biggest asset is the ability to laugh at yourself. You love the sun and don't do well in a damp climate. Hot saunas would give you the tonic you need in the depths of winter.

STRENGTHS
Carefree and
determined

WEAKNESSES
An attention seeker,
imperious

MEDITATION
*The smallest good deed
is better than the grandest
intention.*

22 August

*Y*ou are an imaginative and single-minded person with a colourful personality. You are very receptive to people. You have a fertile imagination and create vivid pictures with words or images of the world you see. You translate your impressions into an art form that has the capacity to touch people's hearts. You are very sociable and possess the gift of creating a warm and vibrant atmosphere around you. You care for people deeply and keep in close contact with your family. You need to have a mate, because without one you feel incomplete. You make a devoted partner and parent. But because you express yourself with your whole heart, you are emotionally vulnerable. If you feel attacked, you are prone to stomach upsets. Chamomile or peppermint teas are better for you than caffeine.

STRENGTHS
Creative,
strong-minded

WEAKNESSES
Insecure and
oversensitive

MEDITATION
*Put your future in good
hands — your own.*

23 August

You are a hard-working person with a playful child inside you that just has to be expressed. With your innate artistic flair you are dedicated to being the best at what you do, and will practice laboriously to perfect any weakness. Your nature is to be useful but there is also a part of you that loves showing off – although this is just a mask for your self-consciousness. In relationships you crave appreciation and to be recognized for your talent. If your partner neglects to do this, you can sulk. However, you cannot be pushed into the spotlight and at times you can be shy and excessively modest. This ambivalence can make it difficult for people to know where they stand. Winter isn't a good time for you. You need sunshine. Taking a short break somewhere hot will restore your spirits at this time of year.

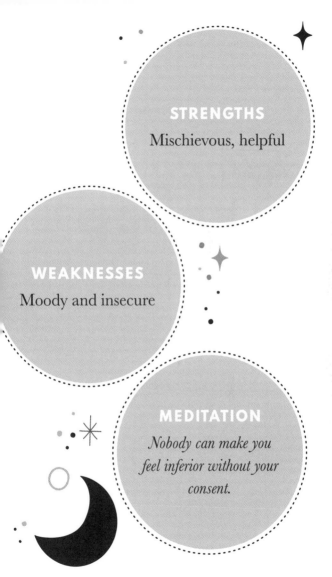

STRENGTHS
Mischievous, helpful

WEAKNESSES
Moody and insecure

MEDITATION
Nobody can make you feel inferior without your consent.

Going
DEEPER

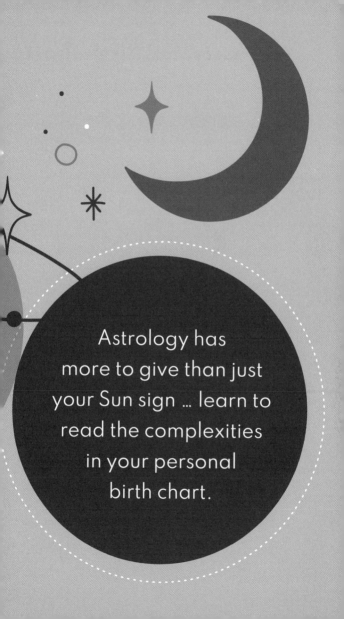

Astrology has more to give than just your Sun sign ... learn to read the complexities in your personal birth chart.

Your personal birth chart

*U*nderstanding your Sun sign is an essential part of astrology, but it's the tip of the iceberg. To take your astrological wisdom to the next level, you'll need a copy of your unique birth chart – a map of the heavens for the precise moment you were born. You can find your birth chart at the Free Horoscopes link at: www.astro.com.

ASTROLOGICAL SYNTHESIS

When you first explore your chart, you'll find that as well as a Sun sign, you also have a Moon sign, plus a Mercury, Venus, Mars, Jupiter, Saturn, Neptune, Uranus and Pluto sign – and that they all mean something different. Then there are astrological houses to consider, ruling planets and Rising signs, aspects and element types – all of which you will learn more about in the birth chart section on pages 112–115.

The art to astrology is in synthesising all this intriguing information to paint a picture of someone's character, layer by layer. Now that you understand your Leo Sun personality better, it's time to go deeper, and to look at the next layer – your Moon sign. To find your own Moon sign go to pages 104–111.

THE MOON'S INFLUENCE

After the Sun, your Moon sign is the second biggest astrological influence in your birth chart. It describes your emotional nature – your feelings, instincts and moods and how you respond to different sorts of people and situations. By blending your outer, Leo Sun character with your inner, emotional, Moon sign, you'll get a much more balanced picture. If you don't feel that you're 100% Leo, your Moon sign will probably explain why!

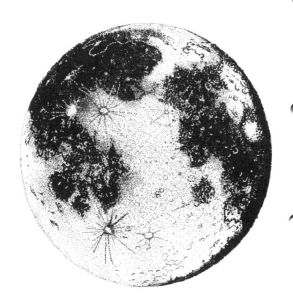

Leo with Moon signs

LEO SUN/**ARIES MOON**

 You're an intense, passionate individual with an incredible sense of purpose. You're bright and impulsive, always ready to give 100% to whatever's in front of you. You are a passionate and generous lover, especially at the beginning of a relationship and you are best suited to other Fire or Air Moon signs for emotional compatibility. You need space to grow, and plenty of enthusiasm from your other half. As an active, energetic person, you adore a new challenge but that also means you can get bored with other projects before you've finished with them. Your temper can be a little wild sometimes, but it usually blows over as quickly as it began – and, thankfully, you don't hold grudges.

LEO SUN/**TAURUS MOON**

 A strong, honest individual, your Taurus Moon gifts you with extra staying power and determination. You take things slower than your average Leo, and you can get on with things on your own, rather than needing to perform for an audience. You have leadership qualities and excellent people skills. The Taurus love of art and music is strengthened by your Leo Sun, and you're probably a skilled artist or have exceptional musical ability. It's important for you to build something of lasting value in your life, and with your creative Leo Sun that probably means something pretty spectacular. You can be a little possessive of the people around you, and a little bossy, but your loved ones usually understand that you have their best interests at heart!

LEO SUN/**GEMINI MOON**

 People don't come much more fun than extravagant Leo with bubbly Gemini Moons! You're a cheerful, warm person, always curious about what everyone else is doing. The life of any social gathering, you're happiest when surrounded by people, especially if they need your advice or opinions. Romantically, you crave variety and plenty of communication. You're an active person and need to experience the world around you in as exciting a way as possible. You're no couch potato and finding a partner that shares your energetic, light-hearted philosophy is crucial. You can find it difficult to relax and aren't always keen to spend time on your own. You get your energy from other people and thrive in a relationship where you share a lively social life.

LEO SUN/**CANCER MOON**

More introspective than your average Leo, your moods change frequently, reflecting the different phases of the Moon. You're not one for night clubs, casinos and glitz and glamour, but you take entertaining at home to a different level. A house full of friends, pets and family is a happy one to you, and it's where you are most relaxed.

Your Cancer Moon counts the pennies, but your Leo Sun is a big spender – and these two sides of your nature may jostle for top position. You need a reassuring, emotionally strong partner who puts you at the centre of their life. You long to feel appreciated and loved and as a loyal and generous partner, will shower your beloved with affection.

LEO SUN/**LEO MOON**

Born at a new Moon, you're a double Leo! All the qualities of Leo are magnified here, and you'll let nothing stand in your way of success. You are wonderfully creative with extravagant taste, which colours everything you do with glamour and drama. You're slightly impatient with less talented or gregarious individuals, and you tend to think doing things your way is the only option. You need a partner you can admire and who knows how to handle your double-Fire energy. You can be dominant and bossy, but you're also very dependent on other people's approval so your partner will see a more insecure side of your personality. You demand loyalty and respect from your friends and family who know underneath all your bluff and bluster that you're actually just a cute little pussycat.

LEO SUN/**VIRGO MOON**

Your bold, flashy Leo ego is tempered by a modest Virgo Moon, which is considerably shyer and more modest. With this extremely well-organised combination you can look at any complicated mess and know instantly how to tidy it up and make it work. The usual Leo disregard for details works well here as your Virgo Moon knows how to make all the little parts come together for your Leo Sun's grander picture. Staying fit and healthy will be especially important, and a partner who enjoys healthy cooking and looking as good as you, will be welcomed. You may need to curb your tendency to criticize yourself and learn how to love all your idiosyncrasies.

LEO SUN/**LIBRA MOON**

With your exuberant Leo Sun and charming Libra Moon, making a good impression on other people is important. Your glamorous Sun and refined Moon suggest you love dressing up and looking the part. Even your dog-walking clothes are stylish or striking. You're probably a little less decisive than the average Leo, as your Moon sees you taking much longer to weigh things up before deciding what to do. This indecisiveness can also apply to romance, where working out what you want from a partner can be a challenge. With a taste for the finer things in life, a lover who is graceful and discerning would be a good start, and a love of the arts would also tick many boxes.

LEO SUN/**SCORPIO MOON**

This is a dynamic, powerful meshing of strong characteristics. Your Leo Sun is bold and brave on the outside – and Scorpio Moon people are passionate and a little ruthless on the inside. Everyone wants to be your friend because nobody wants you as an enemy! You're fiercely loyal to your friends, family and loved ones but can appear indifferent to people who don't know you well. You're a sensual, playful lover but your emotions run deep. When all that intense energy is pointed in a positive direction, you're an incredible force for good. But if you decide against someone or something, you rarely even think about it again. A potential partner would be mindful of your mood shifts and know how to handle the change in temperature!

LEO SUN/**SAGITTARIUS MOON**

This is a gregarious, boisterous pairing – positive, adventure-loving and broad-minded. Finding a partner may be something of a challenge as Sagittarius Moon people don't usually want to settle down early. The world is out there waiting for you, and you want to dive in at the deep end. Emotionally you need space and freedom to do your own thing. Your warmth, generosity and big personality attract people to you easily – you're not exactly a wallflower. You're a little out of your comfort zone dealing with challenging emotions – other people's and your own. Your instinct is to trust that a positive attitude will be enough to get your through, and it usually is!

LEO SUN/**CAPRICORN MOON**

Capricorn's determination tames your overly-enthusiastic Leo Sun and slows you down a little. You're slightly more practical than a typical idealistic Leo, but your ambitions and courage know no bounds. You enjoy socialising with your closest friends but you're not usually a party animal. You are reliable and resourceful, and your reputation is important. You may be a little status-conscious too, with ostentatious preferences for flashy cars, a luxury home and sometimes a high-profile partner. Your other half will need to be sympathetic to your ambitious nature and able to spot when you're feeling out of sorts. Sometimes your Capricorn Moon can get a little blue, but an emotionally intelligent partner will help coax you back to your sunnier side.

LEO SUN/AQUARIUS MOON

You were born on a full Moon, when the Sun was in the opposite sign of the zodiac to your Moon. Opposing signs often produce very independent, self-sufficient people who have had to overcome more challenges than most. Staying focused can be a challenge because you are interested in so many different ideas. You have a unique sense of style and others may occasionally label you as eccentric. But you're just confident about expressing who you really are. Your love life may be unusual too, and you may decide upon an unconventional relationship. You're not really interested in the traditional tried-and-tested approach – you want to break new ground – and need a broad-minded partner in crime to join you!

LEO SUN/PISCES MOON

Pisces Moons are private, quiet people who enjoy tranquil surroundings, which doesn't quite fit with your average loud, proud Leo! But your thoughtful and empathic nature makes you a very popular person. You're encouraging and sympathetic and have a vivid imagination. Leo can be easily hurt if they feel ignored and your gentle Pisces nature, magnifies this sensitivity. Your love life may have already tossed you some curveballs, but your proud Leo confidence means you won't let yourself stay downhearted for very long. You're an optimist at heart and have an unshakeable belief that the Universe is a benevolent place – and that you deserve to be happy. This ability to bounce back will attract other positive, happy people to you.

Birth charts

*L*earning about your Sun and Moon sign opens the gateway into exploring your own birth chart. This snapshot of the skies at the moment of someone's birth is as complex and interesting as the person it represents. Astrologers the world over have been studying their own birth charts, and those of people they know, their whole lives and still find something new in them every day. There are many schools of astrology and an inexhaustible list of tools and techniques, but here are the essentials to get you started ...

ZODIAC SIGNS AND PLANETS

These are the keywords for the 12 zodiac signs and the planets associated with them, known as ruling planets.

 ARIES
courageous, bold, aggressive, leading, impulsive

Ruling planet
 MARS
shows where you take action and how you channel your energy

TAURUS
reliable, artistic, practical, stubborn, patient

Ruling planet
VENUS
describes what you value and who and what you love

GEMINI
clever, friendly, superficial, versatile

Ruling planet
MERCURY
represents how your mind works and how you communicate

CANCER
emotional, nurturing, defensive, sensitive

Ruling planet

MOON
describes your emotional needs and how you wish to be nurtured

LEO
confidence, radiant, proud, vain, generous

Ruling planet
SUN
your core personality and character

VIRGO
analytical, organised, meticulous, thrifty

 Ruling planet
MERCURY
co-ruler of Gemini and Virgo

 LIBRA
fair, indecisive, cooperative, diplomatic

 Ruling planet
VENUS
co-ruler of Taurus and Libra

 SCORPIO
regenerating, magnetic, obsessive, penetrating

 Ruling planet
PLUTO
deep transformation, endings and beginnings

 SAGITTARIUS
optimistic, visionary, expansive, blunt, generous

Ruling planet
JUPITER
travel, education and faith in a higher power

CAPRICORN
ambitious, responsible, cautious, conventional

Ruling planet
SATURN
your ambitions, work ethic and restrictions

AQUARIUS
unconventional, independent, erratic, unpredictable

Ruling planet
URANUS
where you rebel or innovate

PISCES
dreamy, chaotic, compassionate, imaginative, idealistic

Ruling planet
NEPTUNE
your unconscious, and where you let things go

The 12 houses

irth charts are divided into 12 sections, known as houses, each relating to different areas of life as follows:

1 FIRST HOUSE

associated with *Aries*

Identity – how you appear to others and your initial response to challenges

2 SECOND HOUSE

associated with *Taurus*

How you make and spend money, your talents, skills and how you value yourself

3 THIRD HOUSE

associated with *Gemini*

Siblings, neighbours, communication and short distance travel

4 FOURTH HOUSE

associated with *Cancer*

Home, family, your mother, roots and the past

5 FIFTH HOUSE

associated with *Leo*

Love affairs, romance, creativity, gambling and children

SIXTH HOUSE

associated with *Virgo*

Health, routines, organisation and pets

EIGHTH HOUSE

associated with *Scorpio*

Sex, death, transformation, wills and money you share with another

SEVENTH HOUSE

associated with *Libra*

Relationships, partnerships, others and enemies

NINTH HOUSE

associated with *Sagittarius*

Travel, education, religious beliefs, faith and generosity

TENTH HOUSE

associated with *Capricorn*

Career, father, ambitions, worldly success

ELEVENTH HOUSE

associated with *Aquarius*

Friends, groups, ideals and social or political movements

TWELFTH HOUSE

associated with *Pisces*

Spirituality, the unconscious mind, dreams and karma

THE ELEMENTS

Each zodiac sign belongs to one of the four elements – Earth, Air, Fire and Water – and these share similar characteristics, as listed below.

EARTH

Taurus, Virgo, Capricorn

Earth signs are practical, trustworthy, thorough and logical.

AIR

Gemini, Libra, Aquarius

Air signs are clever, flighty, intellectual and charming.

FIRE

Aries, Leo, Sagittarius

Fire signs are active, creative, warm, spontaneous, innovators.

WATER

Cancer, Scorpio, Pisces

Water signs are sensitive, empathic, dramatic and caring.

PLANETARY ASPECTS

The aspects are geometric patterns formed by the planets and represent different types of energy. They are usually shown in two ways – in a separate grid or aspect grid and as the criss-crossing lines on the chart itself. There are oodles of different aspect patterns but to keep things simple we'll just be working with four: conjunctions, squares, oppositions and trines.

CONJUNCTION

0 degrees apart
intensifying

SQUARE

90 degrees apart
challenging

OPPOSITION

180 degrees apart
polarising

TRINE

120 degrees apart
harmonising

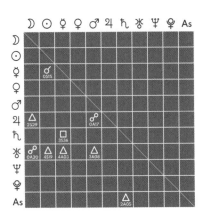

Planetary aspects for Joshua's chart

HOUSES AND RISING SIGN

Each chart is a 360° circle, divided into 12 segments known as the houses (see pages 116–117 for house interpretations). The most important point in a birth chart is known as the Rising sign, which shows the zodiac sign on the Eastern horizon for the moment you were born. This is usually marked as 'As or Asc' on the chart drawing. This is the position from where the other houses and zodiac signs are drawn in a counter-clockwise direction. The Rising sign is always on the dividing line of the first house – the house associated with the self, how you appear to others, and the lens through which you view the world.

CHART RULER: The planetary ruler of a person's Rising zodiac sign is always a key player in unlocking a birth chart and obtaining a deeper understanding of it.

A SIMPLE BIRTH CHART INTERPRETATION FOR A LEO SUN PERSON

BIRTH CHART FOR JOSHUA BORN 11 AUGUST 1985 IN ZAGREB, CROATIA. AT 3.46AM

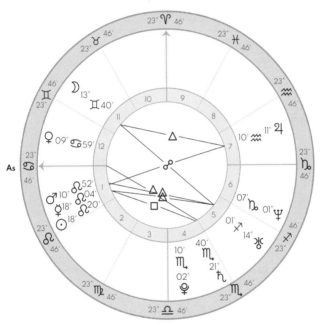

THE POSITION OF THE PLANETS: You can see that Joshua's Sun is in Leo along with Mercury and Mars. He has Cancer Rising, the Moon in Gemini, Venus in Cancer, Jupiter in Aquarius, Saturn and Pluto sit in Scorpio, Uranus occupies Sagittarius and Neptune's in Capricorn.

INTERPRETATION BASICS

As well as checking which sign the planets are in, do also note the house positions of the planets. How do you begin to put all these signs and symbols together? It's usually best to begin with the Sun, Rising sign and then to examine the condition of the Moon sign.

SUN, MOON, RISING SIGN AND CHART RULER: Joshua's Sun – his outer, core personality is Leo in the first house (individuality/the self). The first house is a strong position for the Sun to be in as it's linked with Aries, a Fire sign, just like the Sun. And as Joshua's Sun is in its own sign of Leo, all these Sun/Fire/Leo/Aries factors combine to produce a very capable, enthusiastic, gregarious and brave person.

All this no-holds-barred active energy is at odds with his Cancer (cautious/defensive/sentimental) Rising sign. Perhaps Joshua withholds his emotions when he first meets new people or is a little more thoughtful before he throws himself into new projects. But once he gets going he's a force to be reckoned with.

Joshua's Moon occupies chatty Gemini in the eleventh house of friends and groups; he's probably light-hearted and a bit of a social butterfly at heart. As the ruler of his Cancer Rising sign, Joshua's chart ruler is the Moon, placing further importance on his sociable, talkative side. He's probably rarely bored with all that Gemini curiosity, and enjoys meeting people from all walks of life.

OTHER PLANETS: Mercury, the planet of communication occupies Leo along with Mars and the Sun, and they're in a 'stellium' formation, which is when three planets or more occupy the same area of the chart. This triple conjunction energy magnifies the symbolism of the signs and houses occupied and this Sun (ego), Mars (action), Mercury (communication) all in ebullient Leo, shows someone who is a leader with strong opinions, a super-confident soul who is not afraid to put his money where his mouth is!

Venus (love/money) is found in gentle, emotional, home-loving Cancer in the twelfth house (privacy/secrets/spirituality). Maybe Joshua likes his love life and intimate relationships to be less exposed to the outside world than the rest of his outer, more extrovert tendencies.

Jupiter (luck/expansion/travel) was in Aquarius in the seventh house (relationships) when Joshua was born, showing a need to try innovative or unusual approaches to life, especially through his one-to-one partnerships. As Venus rules the seventh house and for Joshua is in the home sign of Cancer, perhaps he has an unusual or rather eccentric home or family set-up. And as both Saturn (structure) and Pluto (power) also fill his fourth house (family/roots/mother figures) we can guess that Joshua's mother – or the women in his family – have a dynamic effect on his personality.

Uranus, the planet of freedom, takes Joshua's fifth house of creativity and enjoyment and the fact that it's in travel-loving, philosophical Sagittarius, shows a love of change and a willingness to explore. Neptune (dissolving/merging) is in his sixth house of work and health, which could be a confusing area for Joshua, or something of a mystery!

ADDING IN THE PLANETARY ASPECTS:

Let's take a brief look at the strongest aspects – the ones with the most exact angles or 'orbs' to the planetary degrees (the numbers next to the planets).

MOON TRINE JUPITER AND OPPOSITE URANUS: Joshua is emotionally (Moon) broad-minded and optimistic (Jupiter) but he can be subject to unpredictable changes in mood (Uranus).

SUN CONJUNCT MERCURY AND TRINE URANUS: Joshua's ego (Sun) is strengthened (conjunction) by his intellect (Mercury) and he uses unconventional methods (Uranus) to get excellent results (trine).

MERCURY SQUARE SATURN AND TRINE URANUS: Joshua's mental exuberance (Mercury) sometimes meets practical (Saturn) challenges (square). But he also has frequent (trine) moments of genius (Uranus).

MARS OPPOSITE JUPITER AND TRINE URANUS: When Joshua wants to do something (Mars) he experiences extreme reactions (polarising) but when he adopts an unconventional approach (Uranus) he usually gets what he wants (trine)

SATURN TRINE RISING SIGN (AS): Saturn (structure/responsibility) lends Joshua a sense of authority that he radiates to other people (Rising). This position also suggests he's an ambitious and determined person.

YOUR JOB AS AN ASTROLOGER

The interpretation above is simplified to help you understand some of the nuts and bolts of interpretation. There are almost as many techniques and tools for analysing birth charts as there are people!

Remember when you're putting the whole thing together that astrology doesn't show negatives or positives. The planets represent potential and opportunities, rather than definitions set in stone. It's your job as an astrologer to use the planets' wisdom to blend and synthesise those energies to create the picture of a whole person.

Going deeper

To see your own birth chart visit: www.astro.com and click the Free Horoscopes link and then enter your birth information. If you don't know what time you were born, put in 12.00pm. Your Rising sign and the houses might not be right, but the planets will be in the correct zodiac signs and the aspects will be accurate.

Further reading and credits

WWW.ASTRO.COM

This amazing astrological resource is extremely popular with both experienced and beginner astrologers. It's free to sign up and obtain your birth chart and personalised daily horoscopes.

BOOKS

PARKER'S ASTROLOGY by Derek and Julia Parker (Dorling Kindersley)

THE LITTLE BOOK OF ASTROLOGY by Marion Williamson (Summersdale)

THE BIRTHDAY ORACLE by Pam Carruthers (Arcturus)

THE 12 HOUSES by Howard Sasportas (London School of Astrology)

THE ARKANA DICTIONARY OF ASTROLOGY by Fred Gettings (Penguin)

THE ROUND ART by AJ Mann (Paper Tiger)

THE LUMINARIES by Liz Greene (Weiser)

SUN SIGNS by Linda Goodman (Pan Macmillan)

Marion Williamson is a best-selling astrology author and editor. *The Little Book of Astrology* and *The Little Book of the Zodiac* (Summersdale 2018) consistently feature in Amazon's top 20 astrology books. These were written to encourage beginners to move past Sun signs and delve into what can be a lifetime's study. Marion has been writing about different areas of self-discovery for over 30 years. A former editor of *Prediction* magazine for ten years, Marion had astrology columns in *TVTimes*, *TVEasy*, *Practical Parenting*, *Essentials* and *Anglers Mail* for over ten years. Twitter: @_I_am_astrology

Pam Carruthers is a qualified professional Vedic and Western astrologer and student of *A Course in Miracles*. An experienced Life Coach and Trainer, Pam helps clients discover the hidden patterns that are holding them back in their lives. A consultation with her is a life-enhancing and healing experience. She facilitates a unique transformational workshop 'Healing your Birth Story' based on your birthchart. Based in the UK, Pam has an international clientele.

All images courtesy of Shutterstock and Freepik/Flaticon.com.